Writing Numbers

Trace the numbers.

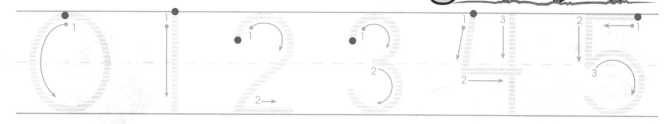

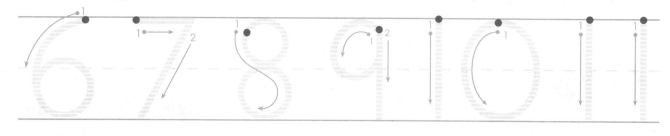

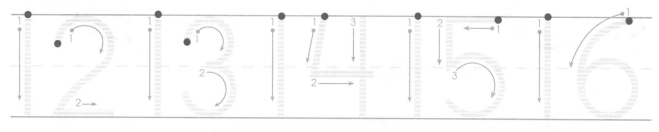

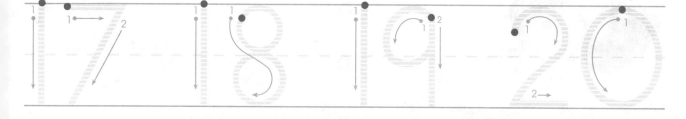

Write the missing numbers.

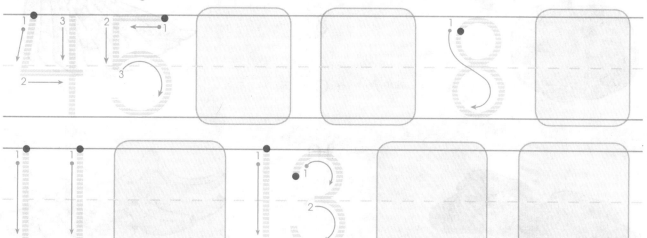

Matching Numbers With Objects

How many vegetables or pieces of fruit are there in each group?
Draw a line from the group to the number.
The first one is done for you.

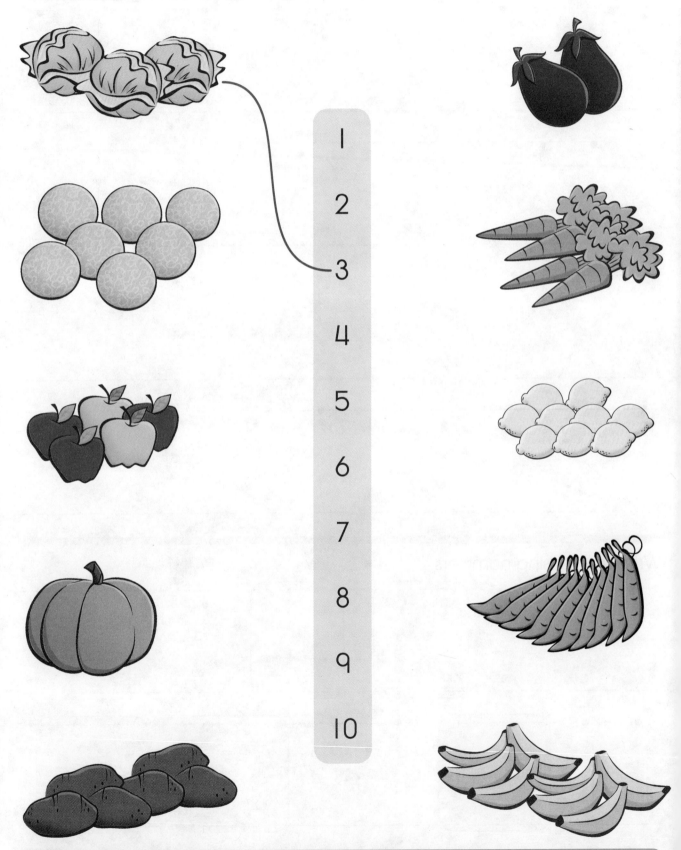

1
2
3
4
5
6
7
8
9
10

Numbers 0 Through 10

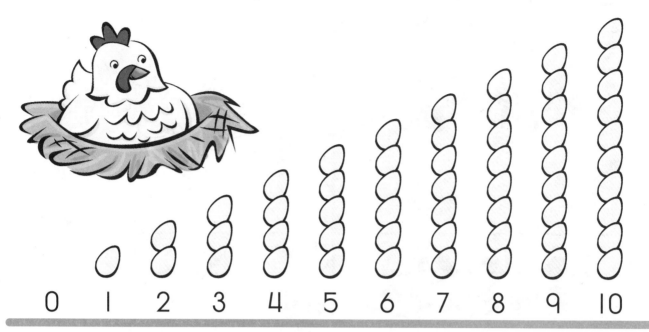

0 1 2 3 4 5 6 7 8 9 10

Circle the number that tells how many chicks there are in each group.

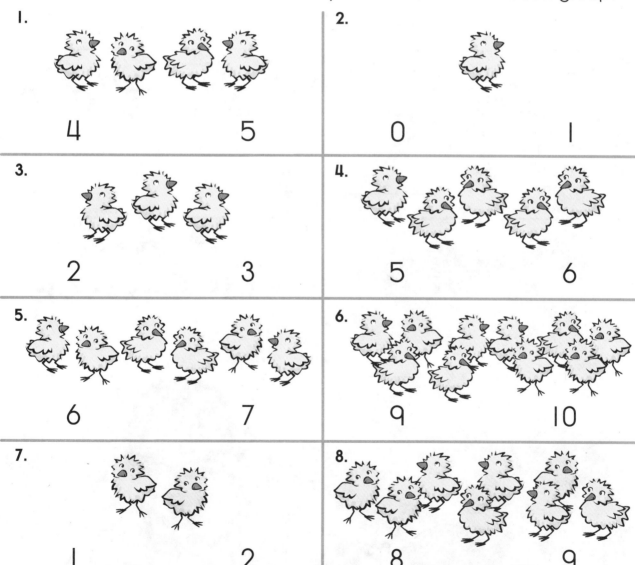

1.

4   5

2.

0   1

3.

2   3

4.

5   6

5.

6   7

6.

9   10

7.

1   2

8.

8   9

Writing Numbers For Objects

Write how many animals there are in each group.

1.

_____

2.

_____

3.

_____

4.

_____

5.

_____

6.

_____

7.

_____

8.

_____

Which Group Has More?

← This group has **more** slices of pie.

Circle the group that has **more** pieces of fruit.

1.

2.

3.

4.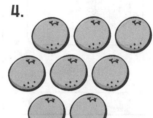

5.

6.

7. Draw a group of to show **2 more** than **3**.

How many did you draw? _____

Concept of *More* (1.NBT.1)

Which Number Is Greater?

$\widehat{5}$ horses

3 horses

5 is **greater** than 3.
Greater means **more than**.

Write how many there are in each group. Circle the **greater** number.

1.

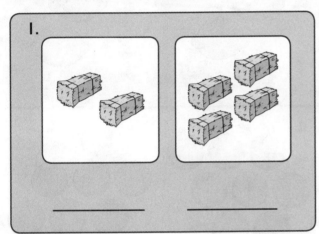

_____   _____

2.

_____   _____

3.

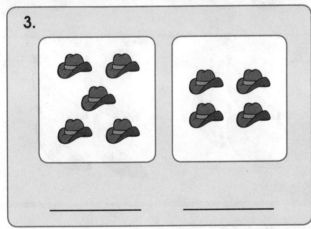

_____   _____

4.

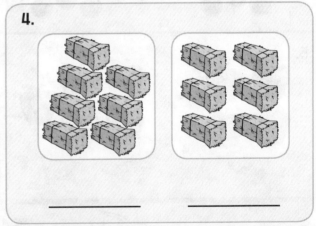

_____   _____

5.

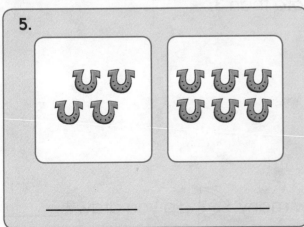

_____   _____

6.

_____   _____

Which Number Is Less?

(8) flowers

9 flowers

8 is **less** than 9.
Less means **fewer** or **not as many**.

Write how many there are in each group. Circle the number that is **less**.

1.

_____   _____

2.

_____   _____

3.

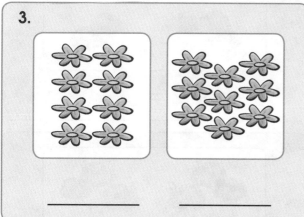

_____   _____

4.

_____   _____

5.

_____   _____

6.

_____   _____

Adding To Find The Sum

The answer to an addition problem is called the **sum**.
You can write an **addition number sentence** like this: **2 + 3 = 5**.

2 + 3 = __5__

Look at the picture. Read the addition number sentence. Write the **sum**.

1.

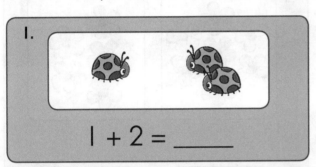

1 + 2 = _____

2.

1 + 1 = _____

3.

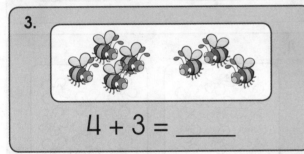

4 + 3 = _____

4.

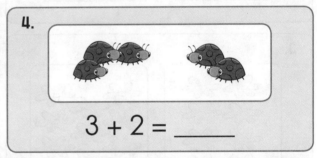

3 + 2 = _____

5.

5 + 1 = _____

6.

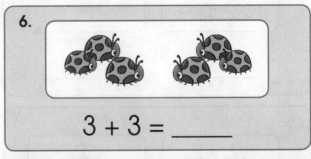

3 + 3 = _____

7.

1 + 4 = _____

8.

2 + 2 = _____

Adding Vertically

```
  1  goat
+ 2  goats
─────
  3  goats ← sum
```

Count the goats. Read the addition problem. Write the **sum**.

1.

```
   2
+  3
─────
```

2.

```
   3
+  1
─────
```

3.
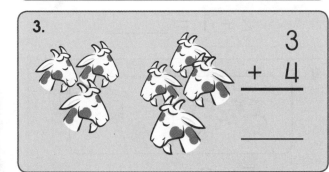
```
   3
+  4
─────
```

4.
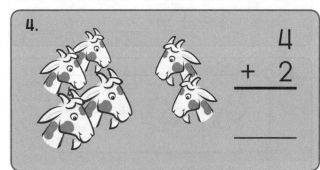
```
   4
+  2
─────
```

5.

```
   2
+  2
─────
```

6.

```
   1
+  3
─────
```

7.

```
   2
+  1
─────
```

8.

```
   6
+  1
─────
```

Subtracting To Find The Difference

The answer to a subtraction problem is called the **difference**.
You can write a **subtraction number sentence** like this: **6 – 2 = 4**.

$$6 - 2 = \underline{4}$$

Count the chicks. Read the subtraction number sentence.
Write the **difference**.

1.

$$3 - 1 = \underline{}$$

2.

$$2 - 1 = \underline{}$$

3.

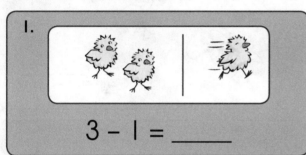

$$4 - 3 = \underline{}$$

4.

$$5 - 2 = \underline{}$$

5.

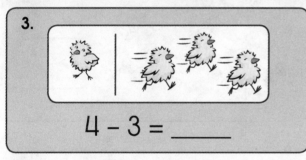

$$6 - 1 = \underline{}$$

6.

$$6 - 2 = \underline{}$$

7.

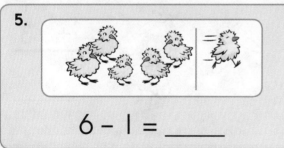

$$7 - 1 = \underline{}$$

8.

$$4 - 2 = \underline{}$$

Subtracting Vertically

3 cows
− 1 cow

$\underline{}$ 2 cows ← **difference**

Count the cows. Read the problem. Write the **difference**.

1.

$$\begin{array}{r} 5 \\ -\ 2 \\ \hline \end{array}$$

2.

$$\begin{array}{r} 4 \\ -\ 1 \\ \hline \end{array}$$

3.

$$\begin{array}{r} 6 \\ -\ 2 \\ \hline \end{array}$$

4.

$$\begin{array}{r} 7 \\ -\ 1 \\ \hline \end{array}$$

5.

$$\begin{array}{r} 4 \\ -\ 3 \\ \hline \end{array}$$

6.

$$\begin{array}{r} 5 \\ -\ 3 \\ \hline \end{array}$$

7.

$$\begin{array}{r} 3 \\ -\ 2 \\ \hline \end{array}$$

8.

$$\begin{array}{r} 6 \\ -\ 1 \\ \hline \end{array}$$

Adding And Subtracting

Read the signs.

The **+** sign tells you to add.

The **−** sign tells you to subtract.

Add   Subtract

$$3$$
$$+2$$
$$\overline{5}$$

$$3$$
$$-2$$
$$\overline{1}$$

Write the **sum** or **difference**.
The addition facts table on page 24 may help you.

1. $3 + 2 =$ _____   2. $4 - 1 =$ _____   3. $5 + 0 =$ _____

4. $6 - 1 =$ _____   5. $2 + 5 =$ _____   6. $4 - 3 =$ _____

7. $7 - 0 =$ _____   8. $2 + 2 =$ _____   9. $4 + 3 =$ _____

10.
$$6$$
$$+1$$

11.
$$3$$
$$-1$$

12.
$$7$$
$$+0$$

13.
$$5$$
$$-1$$

14.
$$4$$
$$-2$$

15.
$$0$$
$$+2$$

16.
$$4$$
$$+2$$

17.
$$3$$
$$-0$$

Finding Sums Through 10

Count all the eggs to find how many there are **in all**.

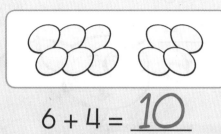

$6 + 4 = \underline{10}$

Count the eggs. Read the addition number sentence. Write the **sum**.

1.

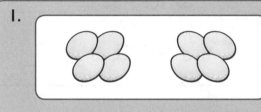

$4 + 4 = \underline{}$

2.

$3 + 6 = \underline{}$

3.

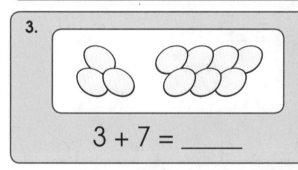

$3 + 7 = \underline{}$

4.

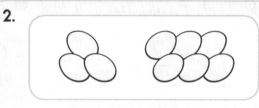

$4 + 5 = \underline{}$

5.

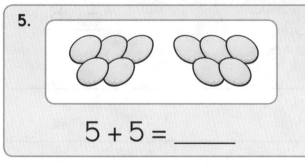

$5 + 5 = \underline{}$

6.

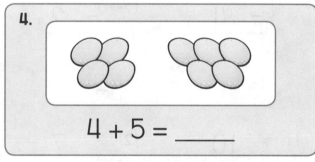

$2 + 6 = \underline{}$

7.

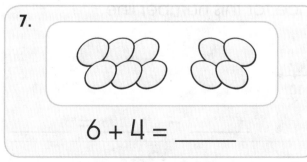

$6 + 4 = \underline{}$

8.

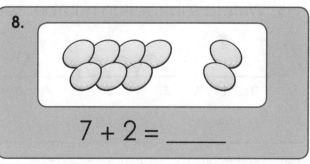

$7 + 2 = \underline{}$

More Subtraction Practice

A number line can help you find the **difference**.

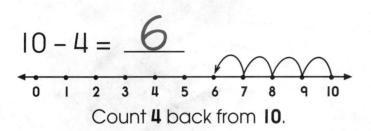

$10 - 4 = \underline{6}$

Count **4** back from **10**.

$$
\begin{array}{r}
10 \\
-\ 4 \\
\hline
6
\end{array}
$$

Write the **difference**.

1. $8 - 3 = \underline{\hphantom{00}}$ 2. $7 - 2 = \underline{\hphantom{00}}$ 3. $10 - 4 = \underline{\hphantom{00}}$

4. $9 - 1 = \underline{\hphantom{00}}$ 5. $6 - 0 = \underline{\hphantom{00}}$ 6. $8 - 4 = \underline{\hphantom{00}}$

7.
$$
\begin{array}{r}
6 \\
-\ 4 \\
\hline
\end{array}
$$

8.
$$
\begin{array}{r}
8 \\
-\ 2 \\
\hline
\end{array}
$$

9.
$$
\begin{array}{r}
5 \\
-\ 5 \\
\hline
\end{array}
$$

10.
$$
\begin{array}{r}
9 \\
-\ 4 \\
\hline
\end{array}
$$

11.
$$
\begin{array}{r}
10 \\
-\ 3 \\
\hline
\end{array}
$$

12.
$$
\begin{array}{r}
7 \\
-\ 4 \\
\hline
\end{array}
$$

13.
$$
\begin{array}{r}
9 \\
-\ 7 \\
\hline
\end{array}
$$

14.
$$
\begin{array}{r}
10 \\
-\ 8 \\
\hline
\end{array}
$$

15. Write a subtraction number sentence for this number line.

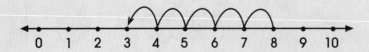

$\underline{\hphantom{000}} - \underline{\hphantom{000}} = \underline{\hphantom{000}}$

Adding And Subtracting

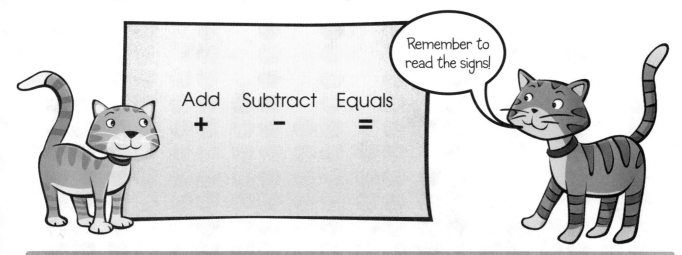

Add   Subtract   Equals

\+   −   =

Remember to read the signs!

Write the **sum** or **difference**.

1. $8 + 1 =$ _____

2. $7 - 2 =$ _____

3. $9 + 0 =$ _____

4. $10 - 1 =$ _____

5. $6 + 3 =$ _____

6. $8 - 3 =$ _____

7. $8 - 0 =$ _____

8. $7 + 2 =$ _____

9. $4 + 6 =$ _____

10. $\begin{array}{r} 1 \\ + 9 \\ \hline \end{array}$

11. $\begin{array}{r} 5 \\ - 1 \\ \hline \end{array}$

12. $\begin{array}{r} 7 \\ + 0 \\ \hline \end{array}$

13. $\begin{array}{r} 9 \\ - 2 \\ \hline \end{array}$

14. $\begin{array}{r} 3 \\ - 0 \\ \hline \end{array}$

15. $\begin{array}{r} 3 \\ + 7 \\ \hline \end{array}$

16. $\begin{array}{r} 5 \\ + 5 \\ \hline \end{array}$

17. $\begin{array}{r} 6 \\ - 0 \\ \hline \end{array}$

Reading Operation Signs (1.OA.6)

Numbers 11 Through 20

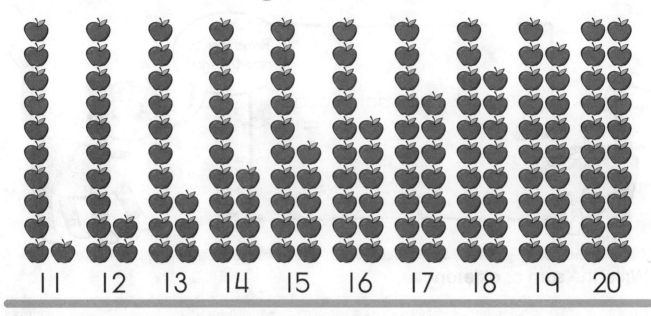

| 11 | 12 | 13 | 14 | 15 | 16 | 17 | 18 | 19 | 20 |

Count the apples. Circle the apples in groups of 10. Then match.
The first one is done for you.

10 and More   **Number**

1.

10 and 3   11

12

2.

10 and 5   13

14

3.

10 and 2   15

4.

10 and 7   16

17

5.

10 and 10   18

19

6.

10 and 6   20

Finding Sums Through 15

$$\underline{5} + \underline{6} = \underline{11}$$

Write an addition number sentence about the eggs.

1.

_____ + _____ = _____

2.

_____ + _____ = _____

3.

_____ + _____ = _____

4.

_____ + _____ = _____

5.

_____ + _____ = _____

6.

_____ + _____ = _____

7.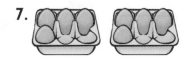

_____ + _____ = _____

8.

_____ + _____ = _____

9.

_____ + _____ = _____

Color the eggs to find the **sum** for the problem. Write the **sum**.

10.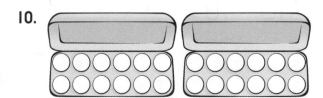

$$7 + 8 = \underline{\hspace{1cm}}$$

11.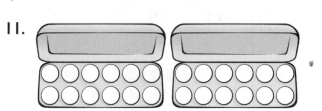

$$7 + 7 = \underline{\hspace{1cm}}$$

More Subtraction Facts

$10 - 7 = \underline{3}$

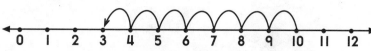

$10 - 3 = \underline{7}$

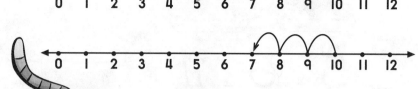

Write the **difference**.

1. $10 - 2 = \underline{\hspace{1cm}}$

   $10 - 8 = \underline{\hspace{1cm}}$

2. $12 - 8 = \underline{\hspace{1cm}}$

   $12 - 4 = \underline{\hspace{1cm}}$

3. $12 - 3 = \underline{\hspace{1cm}}$

   $12 - 9 = \underline{\hspace{1cm}}$

4. $13 - 6 = \underline{\hspace{1cm}}$

   $13 - 7 = \underline{\hspace{1cm}}$

5. $14 - 5 = \underline{\hspace{1cm}}$

   $14 - 9 = \underline{\hspace{1cm}}$

6. $15 - 5 = \underline{\hspace{1cm}}$

   $15 - 10 = \underline{\hspace{1cm}}$

7. $11 - 4 = \underline{\hspace{1cm}}$

   $11 - 7 = \underline{\hspace{1cm}}$

8. $11 - 5 = \underline{\hspace{1cm}}$

   $11 - 6 = \underline{\hspace{1cm}}$

Which Problems Give The Answer?

Circle the problems that equal (=) each number.
The first one is done for you.

1. Circle the problems that equal **9**.

   (10 – 1)   (2 + 7)   (8 + 1)   3 + 5   11 – 3

2. Circle the problems that equal **15**.

   13 + 2   14 – 1   12 + 2   15 – 0   10 + 5

3. Circle the problems that equal **8**.

   10 – 2   4 + 4   6 + 3   2 + 6   12 – 6

4. Circle the problems that equal **10**.

   12 – 3   6 + 4   7 + 3   4 + 5   11 – 1

5. Circle the problems that equal **12**.

   4 + 7   12 – 0   8 + 4   7 + 5   6 + 5

6. Circle the problems that equal **14**.

   11 + 3   15 – 1   9 + 5   10 + 3   7 + 6

7. Circle the problems that equal **11**.

   6 + 4   9 + 2   5 + 6   12 – 2   8 + 3

8. Circle the problems that equal **13**.

   14 + 2   10 + 4   11 + 2   12 + 1   15 – 2

Finding Sums Through 18

$$\begin{array}{r} 9 \\ + 7 \\ \hline 16 \end{array}$$

Write the **sum**.

1. $\begin{array}{r} 8 \\ + 5 \\ \hline \end{array}$
2. $\begin{array}{r} 9 \\ + 9 \\ \hline \end{array}$
3. $\begin{array}{r} 9 \\ + 6 \\ \hline \end{array}$
4. $\begin{array}{r} 8 \\ + 4 \\ \hline \end{array}$

5. $\begin{array}{r} 7 \\ + 6 \\ \hline \end{array}$
6. $\begin{array}{r} 5 \\ + 9 \\ \hline \end{array}$
7. $\begin{array}{r} 7 \\ + 9 \\ \hline \end{array}$
8. $\begin{array}{r} 6 \\ + 6 \\ \hline \end{array}$

9. $\begin{array}{r} 6 \\ + 8 \\ \hline \end{array}$
10. $\begin{array}{r} 7 \\ + 5 \\ \hline \end{array}$
11. $\begin{array}{r} 4 \\ + 9 \\ \hline \end{array}$
12. $\begin{array}{r} 10 \\ + 7 \\ \hline \end{array}$

13. $\begin{array}{r} 7 \\ + 4 \\ \hline \end{array}$
14. $\begin{array}{r} 9 \\ + 0 \\ \hline \end{array}$
15. $\begin{array}{r} 7 \\ + 8 \\ \hline \end{array}$
16. $\begin{array}{r} 5 \\ + 5 \\ \hline \end{array}$

More Subtraction Facts

Think of an addition fact to help you find the **difference**.

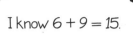

I know $6 + 9 = 15$.

$15 - 6 = \underline{9}$

Write the **difference**.

1. $11 - 7 = \underline{\hspace{1cm}}$ 2. $13 - 9 = \underline{\hspace{1cm}}$ 3. $12 - 5 = \underline{\hspace{1cm}}$

4. $15 - 9 = \underline{\hspace{1cm}}$ 5. $10 - 9 = \underline{\hspace{1cm}}$ 6. $14 - 7 = \underline{\hspace{1cm}}$

7. $12 - 3 = \underline{\hspace{1cm}}$ 8. $15 - 8 = \underline{\hspace{1cm}}$ 9. $13 - 8 = \underline{\hspace{1cm}}$

10. $14 - 5 = \underline{\hspace{1cm}}$ 11. $13 - 6 = \underline{\hspace{1cm}}$ 12. $7 - 0 = \underline{\hspace{1cm}}$

13. $12 - 8 = \underline{\hspace{1cm}}$ 14. $9 - 9 = \underline{\hspace{1cm}}$ 15. $14 - 9 = \underline{\hspace{1cm}}$

16. $17 - 7 = \underline{\hspace{1cm}}$ 17. $18 - 1 = \underline{\hspace{1cm}}$ 18. $16 - 1 = \underline{\hspace{1cm}}$

Differences Related to Sums through 18 (1.OA.6)

Finding Sums Through 20

Here are six addition facts to remember:

$8 + 8 = \underline{16}$ $\quad 8 + 9 = \underline{17}$

$9 + 7 = \underline{16}$ $\quad 9 + 9 = \underline{18}$

$9 + 10 = \underline{19}$ $\quad 10 + 10 = \underline{20}$

Write the **sum**.

1. $8 + 7 = \underline{\hspace{1cm}}$ 　　2. $8 + 8 = \underline{\hspace{1cm}}$ 　　3. $8 + 9 = \underline{\hspace{1cm}}$

4. $7 + 7 = \underline{\hspace{1cm}}$ 　　5. $7 + 8 = \underline{\hspace{1cm}}$ 　　6. $7 + 9 = \underline{\hspace{1cm}}$

7. $9 + 7 = \underline{\hspace{1cm}}$ 　　8. $9 + 8 = \underline{\hspace{1cm}}$ 　　9. $9 + 9 = \underline{\hspace{1cm}}$

10. $8 + 10 = \underline{\hspace{1cm}}$ 　11. $9 + 10 = \underline{\hspace{1cm}}$ 　12. $10 + 10 = \underline{\hspace{1cm}}$

13.
$$\begin{array}{r} 8 \\ + 5 \\ \hline \end{array}$$

14.
$$\begin{array}{r} 6 \\ + 7 \\ \hline \end{array}$$

15.
$$\begin{array}{r} 9 \\ + 6 \\ \hline \end{array}$$

16.
$$\begin{array}{r} 10 \\ + 9 \\ \hline \end{array}$$

17.
$$\begin{array}{r} 9 \\ + 8 \\ \hline \end{array}$$

18.
$$\begin{array}{r} 9 \\ + 7 \\ \hline \end{array}$$

19.
$$\begin{array}{r} 6 \\ + 8 \\ \hline \end{array}$$

20.
$$\begin{array}{r} 9 \\ + 9 \\ \hline \end{array}$$

Addition Number Wheels

Fill in each addition number wheel.
Add the number in the center to each number in the middle.
The first one is done for you.

Wheel 1 (center 9):
- 9 → 18
- 5
- 0
- 8
- 6
- 3

Wheel 2 (center 8):
- 5
- 9
- 8
- 4
- 7
- 6

Wheel 3 (center 10):
- 0
- 2
- 4
- 6
- 8
- 10

Wheel 4 (center 7):
- 9
- 7
- 3
- 2
- 8
- 4

Adding – Sums through 20 (1.OA.8)

Addition Facts Table–Sums Through 20

Write the **sum** in each box to fill in the addition facts table.

+	0	1	2	3	4	5	6	7	8	9	10
0	0			3							
1								8			
2			4								
3											
4						9					
5									13		
6	6										
7					11						
8											
9			11			14					
10											

Each of these addition facts can be called a **double**.
Write the **sum**.

1. $1 + 1 =$ _____

2. $2 + 2 =$ _____

3. $3 + 3 =$ _____

4. $4 + 4 =$ _____

5. $5 + 5 =$ _____

6. $6 + 6 =$ _____

7. $7 + 7 =$ _____

8. $8 + 8 =$ _____

9. $9 + 9 =$ _____

Tens And Ones

_____1_____ ten _____1_____ one

How many? ___11___

Count the vegetables. Circle the vegetables in groups of ten.
Write how many **tens** and **ones** there are. Then write the number.

1.

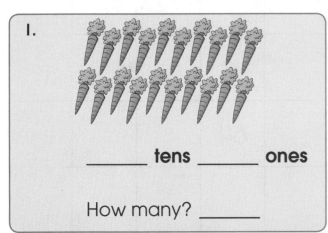

_____ tens _____ ones

How many? _____

2.

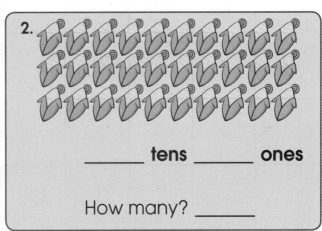

_____ tens _____ ones

How many? _____

3.

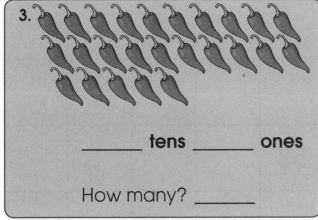

_____ tens _____ ones

How many? _____

4.

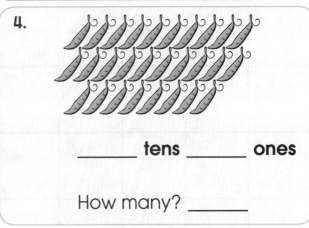

_____ tens _____ ones

How many? _____

5.

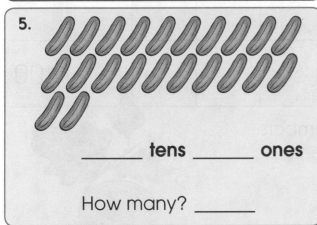

_____ tens _____ ones

How many? _____

6.

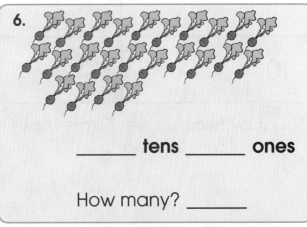

_____ tens _____ ones

How many? _____

Let's Count To 100!

Count to **100**.
Write the missing numbers.

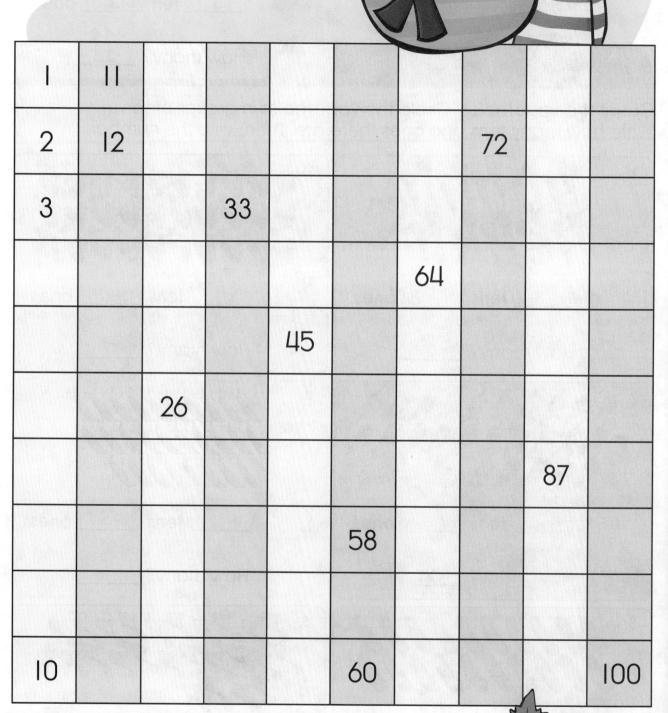

1	11								
2	12						72		
3		33							
				64					
			45						
	26								
						87			
				58					
10				60					100

Count by **twos** above. Circle those numbers.

Counting To 100

Write the missing numbers.

1. 1, 2, _____, 4, 5, _____, 7, _____, _____, 10

2. 41, _____, _____, _____, 45, 46, _____, 48, _____, 50

3. _____, 72, 73, _____, 75, _____, _____, 78, _____, _____

4. 31, _____, _____, _____, 35, _____, 37, _____, _____

5. _____, _____, 83, _____, _____, _____, _____, 88, _____, 90

6. 61, _____, _____, _____, _____, _____, _____, _____, 69

7. 92, _____, 94, _____, _____, _____, _____, 99, _____

Numerical Order (1.NBT.1)

Greater Than And Less Than

(42)   24   42 is **greater** than 24.

Circle the number in each pair that is **greater**.
The first one is done for you.

1. (23)	14		2. 50	48		3. 25	31
4. 19	21		5. 35	27		6. 10	15
7. 18	10		8. 13	31		9. 43	34

Circle the number in each pair that is **less**.
The first one is done for you.

10. 55	(48)		11. 25	31		12. 23	36
13. 62	59		14. 18	13		15. 98	99
16. 58	69		17. 44	54		18. 78	82

What I Learned About Numbers

Write **how many** there are in each group.

1.

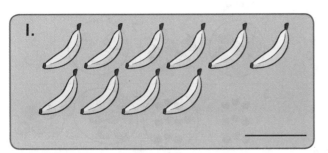

_____

2.

_____

Circle groups of ten. Count the ones. Write **how many** there are.

3.

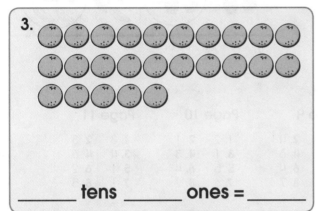

_____ **tens** _____ **ones** = _____

4.

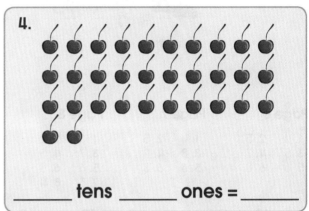

_____ **tens** _____ **ones** = _____

5. Count the pieces of fruit in each group.
Write the numbers. Circle the number that is **less**.

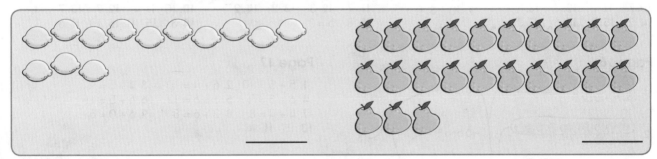

_____   _____

Circle the number that is **greater** in each pair.

6. 29   37   **7.** 41   31   **8.** 69   70

Write the missing numbers.

9. 31, ____, 33, ____, ____, ____, 37, ____, 39, ____

10. 75, ____, ____, 78 ____, ____, 81, ____, ____, 84

Answer Key

Page 1

4, 5, 6, 7, 8, 9
11, 12, 13, 14, 15

Page 2

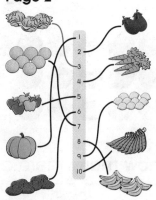

Page 3

1. 4   2. 1
3. 3   4. 5
5. 6   6. 10
7. 2   8. 8

Page 4

1. 4   2. 9
3. 6   4. 3
5. 7   6. 10
7. 5   8. 8

Page 5

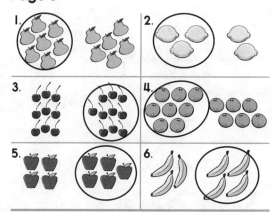

7.
5

Page 6

1. 4   2. 5
3. 5   4. 7
5. 6   6. 8

Page 7

1. 4   2. 5
3. 8   4. 9
5. 6   6. 3

Page 8

1. 3   2. 2
3. 7   4. 5
5. 6   6. 6
7. 5   8. 4

Page 9

1. 5   2. 4
3. 7   4. 6
5. 4   6. 4
7. 3   8. 7

Page 10

1. 2   2. 1
3. 1   4. 3
5. 5   6. 4
7. 6   8. 2

Page 11

1. 3   2. 3
3. 4   4. 6
5. 1   6. 2
7. 1   8. 5

Page 12

1. 5   2. 3   3. 5
4. 5   5. 7   6. 1
7. 7   8. 4   9. 7
10. 7   11. 2   12. 7   13. 4
14. 2   15. 2   16. 6   17. 3

Page 13

1. 8   2. 9
3. 10   4. 9
5. 10   6. 8
7. 10   8. 9

Page 14

1. 5   2. 5   3. 6
4. 8   5. 6   6. 4
7. 2   8. 6   9. 0   10. 5
11. 7   12. 3   13. 2   14. 2
15. 8 − 5 = 3

Page 15

1. 9   2. 5   3. 9
4. 9   5. 9   6. 5
7. 8   8. 9   9. 10
10. 10   11. 4   12. 7   13. 7
14. 3   15. 10   16. 10   17. 6

Page 16

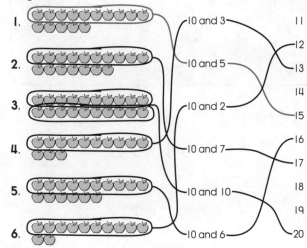

Page 17

1. 5 + 5 = 10   2. 6 + 4 = 10   3. 4 + 5 = 9
4. 6 + 3 = 9   5. 6 + 6 = 12   6. 6 + 5 = 11
7. 4 + 4 = 8   8. 2 + 6 = 8   9. 6 + 0 = 6
10. 15   11. 14

Page 18

1. 8   2. 4
    2   8
3. 9   4. 7
    3   6
5. 9   6. 10
    5   5
7. 7   8. 6
    4   5

Page 19

1. 10 − 1, 2 + 7, 8 + 1
2. 13 + 2, 15 − 0, 10 + 5
3. 10 − 2, 4 + 4, 2 + 6
4. 6 + 4, 7 + 3, 11 − 1
5. 12 − 0, 8 + 4, 7 + 5
6. 11 + 3, 15 − 1, 9 + 5
7. 9 + 2, 5 + 6, 8 + 3
8. 11 + 2, 12 + 1, 15 − 2

Answer Key

Page 20

1. 13 2. 18 3. 15 4. 12
5. 13 6. 14 7. 16 8. 12
9. 14 10. 12 11. 13 12. 17
13. 11 14. 9 15. 15 16. 10

Page 21

1. 4 2. 4 3. 7
4. 6 5. 1 6. 7
7. 9 8. 7 9. 5
10. 9 11. 7 12. 7
13. 4 14. 0 15. 5
16. 10 17. 17 18. 15

Page 22

1. 15 2. 16 3. 17
4. 14 5. 15 6. 16
7. 16 8. 17 9. 18
10. 18 11. 19 12. 20
13. 13 14. 13 15. 15 16. 19
17. 17 18. 16 19. 14 20. 18

Page 23

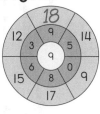
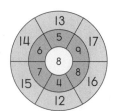
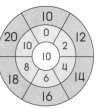
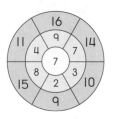

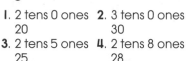

Page 24

+	0	1	2	3	4	5	6	7	8	9	10
0	0	1	2	3	4	5	6	7	8	9	10
1	1	2	3	4	5	6	7	8	9	10	11
2	2	3	4	5	6	7	8	9	10	11	12
3	3	4	5	6	7	8	9	10	11	12	13
4	4	5	6	7	8	9	10	11	12	13	14
5	5	6	7	8	9	10	11	12	13	14	15
6	6	7	8	9	10	11	12	13	14	15	16
7	7	8	9	10	11	12	13	14	15	16	17
8	8	9	10	11	12	13	14	15	16	17	18
9	9	10	11	12	13	14	15	16	17	18	19
10	10	11	12	13	14	15	16	17	18	19	20

1. 2 2. 4 3. 6
4. 8 5. 10 6. 12
7. 14 8. 16 9. 18

Page 25

1. 2 tens 0 ones 2. 3 tens 0 ones
   20   30
3. 2 tens 5 ones 4. 2 tens 8 ones
   25   28
5. 2 tens 2 ones 6. 2 tens 4 ones
   22   24

Page 26

1	11	21	31	41	51	61	71	81	91
2	12	22	32	42	52	62	72	82	92
3	13	23	33	43	53	63	73	83	93
4	14	24	34	44	54	64	74	84	94
5	15	25	35	45	55	65	75	85	95
6	16	26	36	46	56	66	76	86	96
7	17	27	37	47	57	67	77	87	97
8	18	28	38	48	58	68	78	88	98
9	19	29	39	49	59	69	79	89	99
10	20	30	40	50	60	70	80	90	100

Page 27

1. 1, 2, 3, 4, 5, 6, 7, 8, 9, 10
2. 41, 42, 43, 44, 45, 46, 47, 48, 49, 50
3. 71, 72, 73, 74, 75, 76, 77, 78, 79, 80
4. 31, 32, 33, 34, 35, 36, 37, 38, 39
5. 81, 82, 83, 84, 85, 86, 87, 88, 89, 90
6. 61, 62, 63, 64, 65, 66, 67, 68, 69
7. 92, 93, 94, 95, 96, 97, 98, 99, 100

Page 28

Greater
1. 23 2. 50 3. 31
4. 21 5. 35 6. 15
7. 18 8. 31 9. 43
Less
10. 48 11. 25 12. 23
13. 59 14. 13 15. 98
16. 58 17. 44 18. 78

Page 29

1. 10 2. 16
3. 2 tens 5 ones = 25 4. 3 tens 2 ones = 32
5. (13) 23
6. 37 7. 41 8. 70
9. 31, 32, 33, 34, 35, 36, 37, 38, 39, 40
10. 75, 76, 77, 78, 79, 80, 81, 82, 83, 84

AWARD

Great Job!

_____
Name

**finished Math Basics 1 from
School Zone Publishing Company.**